The Caucasian Captive: A True Story

Leo Tolstoy

In the interest of creating a more extensive selection of rare historical book reprints, we have chosen to reproduce this title even though it may possibly have occasional imperfections such as missing and blurred pages, missing text, poor pictures, markings, dark backgrounds and other reproduction issues beyond our control. Because this work is culturally important, we have made it available as a part of our commitment to protecting, preserving and promoting the world's literature. Thank you for your understanding.

POPULAR LECTURES
of the
Russian Pedagogic Museum of Military School
Establishments.

THE CAUCASIAN CAPTIVE

a true story

by

Count TOLSTOY.

Translated from Russian.

St.-Petersburg.
Printing Office of M. M. Stassulewitsch, Was. Ostr., 5 line, 28.
1892

The Caucasian Captive.

I.

In one of the Caucasian regiments there was an officer named Gilin. One day he received a letter from home, in which his old mother wrote to him: „I am growing old, and wish to see my beloved son before I die; come to take leave of me. When I am no more, you may again return to your service. I have found a bride for you; she is intelligent and good, and is not without money. If you like her, perhaps you will marry her, and stay here for good".

Gilin thought: „My old mother is certainly growing feeble; I may never see her more; I think I ought to go, and if I take a fancy to the bride, I may indeed marry her".

He then proceeded to the colonel, obtained leave of absence, bade goodbye to his comrades, and, having treated his soldiers to four pails of vodka, he was ready to start.

At that time war was raging in the Caucasus. The roads were not safe either by day or night. Whenever a Russian ventured to some distance from the fortress, the Tartars were sure to kill him or to carry him off to the mountains. It was therefore arranged that twice a week a convoy of soldiers should be sent from fortress to fortress, some of them going in front, others in the rear of the travellers.

It was summer. At dawn of day a caravan had gathered together behind the fortress, and as soon as the convoy of soldiers was ready, they set off on their way. Gilin was on horseback, and the vehicle with his luggage was in the caravan.

They had 25 versts to go. The caravan moved on slowly; now the soldiers would halt, now a wheel would fall off, or a horse would linger, and then all had to wait.

It was already past midday, and the caravan had only got as far as half way. It was dusty and hot; the sun was broiling, and there was no shelter: the road lay in a barren steppe without a single tree or bush.

Gilin rode off to some distance in front, then stopped and waited for the caravan to approach; he now heard a horn played behind: the caravan had halted again. Gilin thought: „Shall I go on by myself without the soldiers? My horse is good; if the Tartars assault me, I can ride away from them; or had I better stay?".

As he was standing and considering, another officer rode up to him; his name was Kostilin. Kostilin said to him:

„Let us go on, Gilin; I am very hungry, and it is fearfully hot! I am so warm, that you might wring out my shirt".

Kostilin was heavy and stout; his face was red and covered with perspiration. Gilin considered a while and then said:

„Is your gun loaded?".

— Yes, it is.

— Well then, let us go! but remember, we must keep together.

And so they proceeded along the road talking and looking about. They were surrounded by a steppe, a large open space stretched out before their eyes.

By and by they came to the end of the steppe, and entered a ravine between two mountains. Gilin said:

"We ought to ascend the mountain and have a look round; it would be easy to assault us here quite unexpectedly".

Kostilin said:

"What's the use of looking round? let us proceed!".

Gilin would not listen to him.

"No", he said, "wait here below, and I shall ride up and look about".

He then turned his horse to the left up the mountain. Gilin's horse was a hunter (he had given 100 roubles for it when it was a foal, and had himself trained it); it dashed up the steep hill as though it had wings. And there, at the top, quite unexpectedly Gilin found himself face to face with mounted Tartars. There were thirty of them. As soon as Gilin saw them, he began to turn his horse back, but the Tartars had seen him also, and hastily rode towards him, taking their rifles out of their cases. Gilin urged his horse down the steep side of the hill, and cried to Kostilin:

"Take out your rifle!".

He inwardly wished his horse might not stumble. "If only I get to the rifle", thought Gilin, "I shall be able to defend myself".

Meanwhile Kostilin, instead of waiting for his companion, as soon as he saw the Tartars, rode off towards the fortress at the greatest possible speed, lashing his horse on its right and left flanks, and raising such a dust, that nothing but the horse's tail was visible.

Gilin now saw that his situation was bad. The rifle was gone, and nothing could be done with only a sabre. He turned his horse back towards the convoy of soldiers, thinking he might yet escape, but six Tartars were just crossing his way. His horse was good, but their horses were still better. He began to pull up, intending to turn back, but his horse's speed was so great, that he could not stop it, and on it rushed straight upon the Tartars. One of them with a red beard, and mounted upon a grey horse, was already quite close to him; he squeaked, grinned, and held his rifle ready.

„I know you well, you devils", thought Gilin, „if you seize me alive, you will put me into a pit and whip me. On no account shall I surrender while there is life in me".

Gilin was not tall, but he was brave. He drew out his sabre, and urged his horse straight upon the redbearded Tartar, thinking: „I shall either mangle him under my horse, or cut him down with my sabre".

Gilin was at the distance of a horse's length from him, when several shots were fired at him from behind, and his horse was wounded; it fell down heavily upon the ground, pressing Gilin's leg under its body.

He tried to get up, but two Tartars were already beside him tying his arms behind him. He made an effort, and threw them off, but three more had already dismounted from their horses, and now began to strike him on the head with the butt ends of their rifles. His sight became dim, and he staggered. The Tartars then seized him, got some spare girths from their saddles, tied his hands behind his back with a Tartar knot, and dragged him towards the saddle. His cap had been knocked off, his boots pulled off; he was searched all over, his money and watch taken away, his clothes torn. Gilin turned to look at his horse. The poor animal was lying on its side as it had fallen with its legs kicking in the air;

there was an open wound in its head, and dark blood was gushing from it, moistening the dust all round.

One of the Tartars came up to the horse, and began to remove the saddle. The horse was still struggling; he took out a dagger, and cut its throat; blood gushed out, the animal gave a shudder, and was dead. The Tartars then removed the saddle and the bridle. The redbearded Tartar mounted his horse; several others lifted Gilin on to the saddle behind him, and secured him with a strap to the Tartar's belt; in this way he was carried off to the mountains.

Gilin was sitting behind the Tartar rocking to and fro, and every now and then involuntarily thrusting his face into the Tartar's back. He saw before him nothing but this stout Tartar's back and his sinewy neck, and also his shaven nape, which looked blue beneath his cap. Gilin had been wounded in the head, and the blood became clotted over his eyes. He could neither adjust himself more comfortably upon the saddle, nor wipe off the blood. His arms had been so tightly bound behind, that he felt a pain in his clavicle.

They proceeded a long time from one mountain to another, crossed a ford, reached a road, and continued their journey in a valley.

Gilin tried to remember the way by which they were proceeding, but his eyes were covered with blood, and he could not turn.

It was beginning to grow dark; they crossed another river, and began to ascend a rocky hill; the smell of smoke was now felt, and the barking of dogs heard. They arrived at a Tartar village. The Tartars dismounted from their horses; their children gathered round Gilin; they squeaked, and made merry, and threw stones at him.

The redbearded Tartar drove the children away; he took

Gilin off the horse, and called a workman. The workman, a Nogay Tartar, had large cheekbones, and was dressed in a shirt, which was so torn, that his chest was bare. His master gave him some orders. The workman brought a footblock: two pieces of oak with iron rings, and a bolt and lock in one ring.

Gilin was now unbound, the footblock was put on, and he was conducted to a shed; here he was thrust in, and the door was shut. Gilin fell down upon some dung; by and by he groped in the dark, and finding a softer place, he lay down.

II.

Gilin scarcely slept at all that night. The nights were short, and he soon saw daylight breaking through a chink. He got up, enlarged the chink, and looked out.

He saw a road leading down hill; to the right stood a hut with two trees close by. A black dog was lying on the threshold, a she-goat with her kids was walking about. A young Tartar woman was ascending the hill; she was dressed in a loose coloured smock, trousers and boots, her head was covered with her kaftan; she was carrying upon her head a large tin pitcher filled with water; she was leading by the hand a shaven Tartar boy with nothing but a shirt on. The woman entered the hut, out of which issued the redbearded Tartar, whom Gilin had seen the day before; he was dressed in a silk undertunic, a silver dagger was hanging at his side, he wore his shoes upon bare feet. A high black sheepskin cap was placed on the back of his head. He came out, stretched himself, and stroked his red beard. He stood a little while, then gave some instructions to the workman, and went away.

By and by two boys passed on horseback; they were going to give their horses a drink. Several other shaven boys ran out; they were all dressed in shirts without breeches; they gathered in a group, approached the shed, took a rod, and tried to push it through the chink. Gilin shouted at them, and they darted off as quickly as their legs could carry them.

Gilin was very thirsty, his throat was dry; he wished somebody would come to him. By and by he heard that the shed was being opened; it was the redbearded Tartar who entered; he was followed by another Tartar; this one was of a shorter stature and dark; his eyes were black and bright, he was ruddy, his little beard was cut; his face was merry, he seemed always laughing. He was still more richty dressed; his blue silk undertunic was trimmed with silver tape; a large silver dagger hung at his waist; he wore red morocco leather shoes, which were also trimmed with silver tape, and over these were other thick shoes; a high white sheepskin cap covered his head.

The redbearded Tartar entered the shed; he said something in an angry tone of voice, and stood leaning against the lintel; he played with his dagger, and looked askance like a wolf at Gilin. Meanwhile the dark one, brisk and lively, as though he was on springs, came up to Gilin, squatted down, grinned, patted him on the shoulder, and began to talk something very rapidly in his own dialect; he winked his eyes, and clacked with his tongue, repeating every now and then:

„Well Russian! well Russian!"

Gilin could not make out anything, and said: „Bring me some water to drink!"

The dark Tartar laughed, and continued repeating: "Well Russian!"

Then Gilin showed with his lips and hands that he was thirsty.

The dark Tartar understood him; he laughed, looked out and called: "Dina!"

A slender girl of about 13 years of age, bearing a great resemblance to the dark Tartar came running up. You could at once see she was his daughter; she also had bright black eyes and a handsome face. She was dressed in a long blue smock with wide sleeves and without a sash. The skirt, front and sleeves were trimmed with red. She wore trousers and shoes, over which was put on another pair with high heels; she had a necklace consisting of Russian silver half roubles; her head was uncovered; there was a ribbon in her black tresses, and small metal plates and a silver rouble were suspended from the ribbon.

Her father said something to her. She ran away and soon returned with a tin pitcher. She offered the water to Gilin, and then squatted down in such a way, that her shoulders were lower than her knees. She sat thus with her eyes wide open, staring at Gilin while he was drinking, as though he were some wild beast.

Gilin handed her back the pitcher, and she darted off like a wild goat. Even her father laughed. He again sent her somewhere. She took the pitcher, ran off, and brought some unleavened bread upon a round wooden tray; she again sat down, and stared at Gilin without taking her eyes off.

The Tartars departed, and shut the door. After a little while the Nogay Tartar entered, and said:

"Heyda, master, heyda!"

He also did not know Russian. Gilin however understood that he wished him to follow.

Gilin left the shed; he could scarcely walk, because the footblock hindered him. He saw a Tartar village consisting of about 10 houses and a Tartar church with a turret. Three saddled horses were standing at one of the houses, and boys were holding them by the bridles. The dark Tartar came out of this house, and motioned Gilin to come in; he was laughing and talking something in his own dialect. Gilin entered the house. It was a decent room with plastered walls. Several particoloured featherbeds were placed against the wall in front; costly carpets covered the side walls; rifles, pistols and sabres, all set in silver, were hanging upon the carpets. In one of the walls there was a small stove on a level with the floor. There was no flooring, but the ground was hard and clean, like a thrashing floor; in the front corner it was covered with felt, over which carpets were spread and soft cushions placed. Several Tartars with shoes on their bare feet were sitting on these carpets: the dark man, the redbearded one and their three guests. They all had cushions hehind their backs, and before them stood a round wooden tray with millet pancakes, melted butter in a cup and some Tartar ale, called *booza*, in a pitcher. They were eating with their hands, which were quite greasy.

The dark Tartar, having ordered to place Gilin at a little distance from them, not on the carpet, but on the bare floor, again took his seat, and began to treat his guests to the pancakes and the booza. The workman pointed Gilin his place, took off his own upper shoes, placed them at the door in a row with the others, and seated himself on the felt nearer to the hosts; he kept looking at them with envy while they were eating.

When the Tartars had finished eating their pancakes, a Tartar woman came in; her head was covered with a kerchief. She took away the butter and pancakes, and brought a large tub and a pitcher with a narrow spout. The Tartars washed their hands, then folded them, kneeled down, and after blowing in all directions they read their prayers. When the prayers were over, they talked a short time in their own dialect. Then one of the guests, a Tartar, turned towards Gilin, and adressed him in Russian.

„You were captured", he said, „by Kasi-Mahomed", pointing to the red Tartar, „and he gave you over to Abdul-Murat", pointing to the dark one. „Abdul-Murat is now your master". Gilin was silent. Now Abdul-Murat began to speak; he pointed to Gilin, laughed, and kept repeating: „Russian soldier, good Russian!" The interpreter said: „He commands you to write home and ask to send a ransom for you. He will set you free as soon as he gets the money".

Gilin considered a while, and then said:

„And what sum does he require?"

The Tartars consulted a short time; the interpreter said:

„Three thousand coins".

„No", said Gilin. „I cannot pay so much".

Then Abdul rose; he began to gesticulate with his hands, and to speak to Gilin, as though he thought Gilin could understand him. The interpreter translated, saying:

„How much will you give?"

After a little consideration Gilin said:

„500 roubles".

Hereupon all the Tartars began talking rapidly together; Abdul shouted at the redhaired Tartar, but this one only half closed his eyes, and clacked with his tongue.

When they had finished talking, the interpreter said:

„500 roubles is too small a ransom. Your master has himself paid 200 roubles for you. Kasi-Mahomed owed him the sum, and Abdul took you for the debt. He does not consent to let you free under 3000 roubles. If you refuse to write home, you will be thrust into a pit and flogged".

"The more timidity I show, the worse it will be", thought Gilin. He rose to his feet, and said:

"Tell him that if he wants to frighten me, I shall not give him a single copeek, nor shall I write home. I have never feared you, dogs, nor shall I ever fear!"

The interpreter translated this, and then they began again talking noisily all together.

At last the dark Tartar came up to Gilin.

"Russian", he said, "djigit, djigit Russian!"

Djigit in their dialect means "brave fellow". Abdul laughed, and said something to the interpreter; the interpreter translated:

"Give a thousand roubles".

Gilin was obstinate: "I shall not give more than 500 roubles. If you kill me, you will get nothing".

After consulting together a little while the Tartars sent off the workman; they now kept looking at Gilin and at the door. The workman soon returned accompanied by a stout man with bare feet and in tattered clothes; he also had a foot block on. Gilin uttered an exclamation as he recognized Kostilin. So he also was seized! When they were placed side by side, they began to relate to one another all that had happened to them; the Tartars looked on in silence. Gilin told what had befallen him; Kostilin related that his horse had stopped, and his gun had flashed in the pan, and that this same Abdul had caught and seized him.

Abdul rose, pointed to Kostilin, and said something. The interpreter translated into Russian saying that they both now belonged to one master, and that he who pays the ransom first will be also set free first.

„You get into a passion", he said to Gilin, but your companion is gentle; he has already written home, and his relations have promised to send five thousand coins. He will now be fed well, and nobody will molest him".

Gilin said:

„My companion may do as he likes; perhaps he is rich, but I am not. I shall abide by what I have said. You may kill me if you wish, but this will be of no profit to you; I shall not ask to send me more than 500 roubles".

There was silence. Suddenly Abdul jumped up, got a case, out of which he took a pen and some paper and ink; he thrust all this into Gilin's hands, and patted him on the shoulder motioning him to write. He consented to take 500 roubles.

„Wait a little", said Gilin to the interpreter, „tell him, that he must feed us well; he must also supply us with decent boots and clothes, and keep us together, it will be more cheerful for us; the footblock must also be taken off". In saying this Gilin looked at the host, and laughed. The host laughed also, and said:

„I shall give you the very best clothes: you shall have a tscherkesska and boots; you shall be fed like princes, and if you wish to be together, you may both live in the shed. But the footblock must not be taken off: you will run away; it may be taken off for the night only. He again patted him on the shoulder saying: „you good written, my good!"

Gilin wrote the letter, but put a wrong address, that it should not reach its destination. He thought: „I shall run off".

Gilin and Kostilin were then taken to the shed; some straw of Indian wheat was brought to them, also some water in a jug, some bread, two tscherkessky and a pair of old worn out boots, which had evidently been pulled off from some dead soldier's feet. The footblocks were taken off for the night, and they were locked up in the shed.

III.

In this way Gilin lived with his companion a whole month. His master continued to be in a merry mood: „You, John, good; me, Abdul, good". However he fed them badly; they received only unleavened bread, made of millet flour in the shape of flat cakes, and sometimes nothing but unbaked paste.

Kostilin wrote home again; he was anxiously expecting the money, and felt depressed. He would sit in the shed all day long, and either count the days, which it would take his letter to reach its destination, or sleep. As to Gilin he knew well that his letter would never arrive, but still he did not send another.

„Where", thought he, „is my mother to get so much money to pay for me? As it is, she has been living mostly upon what I sent her. She will be quite ruined if she sends me 500 roubles. Perhaps with God's help I may yet manage to escape".

In the mean time he continued to look about and to consider how he could run away.

He would walk about in the village whistling, or else sit making dolls out of clay or plaiting wicker baskets. Gilin was a good hand at all kinds of work.

He once made a doll with a nose and with hands and feet; he dressed it in a Tartar smock, and placed it upon the roof.

When the Tartar women went to fetch water, Abdul's daughter Dinka saw the doll, and called to the others. They all set down their pitchers, stared and laughed. Gilin took down the doll, and gave it to them. They laughed, but were afraid to take it. He left the doll, entered the shed, and looked out to see what would happen next.

Dina ran up, looked round, seized the doll, and ran off.

Next morning at break of day Gilin saw Dina come out and stand on the threshold with the doll in her hands. She had already dressed it in red shreds, and she was now rocking it and singing a lullaby to it, as though it was a child. By and by an old woman came out of the hut; she chid her, snatched the doll, broke it, and sent Dina away to do some work.

Gilin made another doll, a still better one, and gave it to Dina. One day Dina brought a pitcher; she placed it on the ground, sat down, and stared at Gilin, laughing and pointing to the pitcher.

„What makes her so merry?" thought Gilin, He took up the pitcher, and began to drink. He had thought it was water, but he found it was milk. He drank it, and said it was very nice. How pleased Dina was!

„Good, John, good!" and then she jumped up, clapped her hands, seized the pitcher, and ran off.

After this she brought him milk every day. The Tartars would sometimes make flat cheeses from goat's milk, and dry them upon their roofs; these cheeses she would also bring to Gilin; and when Abdul had killed a ram, she brought him in her sleeve a piece of mutton. She would bring these things, and run away.

One day there was a great storm, and during a whole hour the rain poured down in torrents. The water in the rivulets became muddy. The ford turned into a rapid river three arshines deep. There were numerous streams running down, and a rumbling noise was heard in the mountains. Gilin asked his master for a knife, cut out a little cylinder, some small boards, made a wheel, and attached two dolls to the two ends.

The girls brought him some shreds in which he dressed the dolls, one of them as a man, the other as a woman; he then placed the wheel in a rivulet; as it turned, the dolls jumped.

All the village assembled: boys, girls and women; the Tartars also came to look, and were much pleased:

„Ay, Russian! ay, John!"

Abdul had a Russian watch which was broken. He called Gilin and showed him the watch. Gilin said:

„Let me mend it for you".

He took it to pieces with his penknife, then put the pieces together again, and the watch began to go.

Abdul was delighted. He made him a present of his old tattered undertunic. Gilin accepted it thinking he might use it to cover himself in the night.

From that time forth Gilin became celebrated as a Jack of all trades. People would come to him from distant villages; some would bring their guns or their pistols to mend, others their watches. His master gave him some tools: pincers, gimlets and a smooth file.

A Tartar happened to fall ill; they came to Gilin, and said: „Come and cure him!" Gilin had no notion about treating diseases. However he went, looked at the sick man, and thought: „Perhaps he will get well of his own accord". He then went into the shed, mixed some sand and water, whispered something over this in the presence of the Tartars, and gave it to the sick man to drink. To his luck the Tartar recovered.

By this time Gilin was beginning to understand their dialect. Some Tartars got used to him, and when they wanted him, they called: „John! John!" but others still looked at him askance.

The redbearded Tartar did not like Gilin. Whenever he saw him, he would always frown and look away, or abuse him. There was also an old man, who did not live in the village, but came from the foot of the mountain. Gilin saw him only when he came to the mosque to pray. He was short, and wore a white towel wound round his cap; his beard and moustaches were cut; they were as white as snow, and his face was wrinkled and as red as a brick. He had a hooked nose, like the beak of a hawk; his eyes were grey and stern, and he had only two tusks in his mouth. He would walk about with his turban on his head, leaning upon a staff and looking about fiercely; as soon as he perceived Gilin he would express displeasure, and turn away.

One day Gilin went down the hill to see where this old man lived. When he had descended by a path, he saw a garden surrounded by a stone wall; behind the wall were visible wild cherries, apricots and a hut with a flat roof. He approached, and saw beehives made of straw and bees flying about and humming. The old man was kneeling down by the beehives doing something to them. Gilin raised himself in order to have a better view, and his foot block rattled. The old man looked round, and made a sudden exclamation; he snatched a pistol from his belt, and fired at Gilin. Gilin had hardly time to hide himself behind a stone.

The old man came to his master to complain. Abdul called Gilin, and said laughing:

„Why did you go to the old man?„

Gilin answered:

„I meant no harm. I only wished to see how he lived".

The master interpreted this.

But the old man was very angry; he hissed and talked something showing his two tusks and pointing to Gilin.

Gilin could not understand all he said; he could only make out that the old man ordered the master to kill the Russians, and not to keep them in the village.

When the old man was gone, Gilin enquired of his master about him. Abdul said:

„He is a great man! He was the first djigit and had slain many Russians; he was wealthy; he had three wives and eight sons. They all lived in one village. The Russians came, destroyed the village, and killed seven of his sons. The only son left went over to the Russians. The old man then also gave himself up to the Russians; he had been living with them about three months when he discovered his son; he killed him with his own hand, and ran away. Since then he has left off fighting; he went to Mecca to pray. This is why he wears a turban. Those who have visited Mecca are called Hadji, and wear a turban. He hates you, Russians. He wants me to kill you, but I cannot do it; I have paid money for you, and besides, I have taken a fancy to you, John, and would not part with you at all, if I had not promised to let you free".

Sayingt his he laughed, and added in Russian:

„You, John, good; me, Abdul, good!"

IV.

Thus a whole month passed. During the day Gilin would walk about in the village, or do some work; as soon as night approached, and all became quiet in the village, he would begin to dig in his shed. It was hard work, because the stones interfered; but he rubbed them with his smooth file, and managed at length to make a hole under the wall large enough for a man to pass through. „Now", he thought, „I must only get well acquainted with this spot in order to know which way to go. The Tartars will never tell me that".

He chose a day when his master had left home, and went in the afternoon beyond the village; he ascended a hill in order to have a look round. Before going off the master had ordered his son to follow Gilin everywhere, and not to let him out of his sight for a single moment. The boy ran after Gilin shouting:

„Do not go! father has prohibited it. I shall call the people!"

Gilin began to persuade him:

„I shall not go far", he said, „I only want to ascend that hill. I must find a herb to cure your people. Come with me, I shall not be able to run away with the footblock on. I promise to make a bow and arrows for you tomorrow".

Thus the boy was prevailed upon, and they went on together. The hill seemed not far off, but it was heavy walking with the footblock on, and it was a tedious journey for Gilin who hardly managed to mount it. At the top of the hill Gilin sat down, and began to survey the spot. To the south, behind his shed, there was a hollow, where a herd of horses was grazing, and where another village was visible; beyond this village there was another hill, a still steeper one, and beyond that yet another, between the hills there were dark forests; and then again hills, higher and higher. The highest mountains were white, like sugar; they were covered with snow. One of these snow mountains was higher than the rest, and had the form of a cap. To the east and to the west were also such mountains; here and there in the ravines smoke was rising from the villages.

„This is all their place", thought Gilin, and turned towards the Russian side.

He saw a river beneath his feet and the village he lived in, surrounded by small gardens. Women were rinsing linen at the river side, and appeared like little dolls. Beyond the village there was a mountain, and farther away two other mountains; they were covered with a forest; between two mountains he saw an even space, and there, far, far away something like smoke was visible. Gilin tried to recollect where he used to see the sun rise and set when he lived at home. He conjectured that there, in that vale, must be his fortress. In that direction then, between those two mountains, must he fly.

The sun was now beginning to set. The snowy mountains were changing their colour from white to red; it was getting dark in the hills; mist was rising from the hollows; and that same vale, where he thought the fortress was situated ,glowed in the sunset like fire. Gilin looked stiil more intently, he fancied he saw something like smoke rising from the chimneys in the valley, and he could not help thinking that this was the Russian fortress.

It had already grown late. The Mollah had cried out. The herd was being driven home; the cows were bellowing.

The boy kept calling Gilin: „come!" but Gilin did not wish to go yet.

At last they returned home. „Well", thought Gilin, „now I know the place, and must run away". He wanted to risk it that very night. The nights were dark, it was the wane of the moon. Unfortunately the Tartars came back that evening. They generally returned in a joyful mood, driving the cattle they had captured; but this time they had not captured anything, and they were returning bringing with them the body of a killed Tartar, the brother of the redbearded man. They were in a very angry mood. They were now going to bury the dead man. Gilin came out to look at their burial ceremony. They wound some linen round the dead body, and without a coffin they bore it beyond the village, and placed it under some planetrees. The Mollah arrived; several old men gathered together; they wound towels round their caps, took off their shoes, and squatted down before the old man.

The Mollah was in front, three old men in turbans were behind him, and behind these were some more Tartars. When they had taken their places, they bowed their heads down, and were silent. The silence lasted some time. Then the Mollah raised his head, and said:

„Allah!" (this means „God"). He said this single word, and then again they all bent down their heads and were silent a long time, sitting motionless. Once more the Mollah raised his head:

„Allah!" and everyone repeated: „Allah!" and again there was silence. The body was lying upon the grass, and they were sitting as motionless as if they too were dead, not one of them stirred. The only sound to be heard was the rustle of leaves upon the plane tree. Then the Mollah read a prayer after which all the people present stood up; the dead man was raised from the ground and carried off to a pit. It was not a common pit, but a hole dug under the earth like a cellar. The dead man was then taken up under the arms and knees, so that his body was doubled, and thus he was softly let down and placed under the ground in a sitting posture with his hands upon his belly.

The Nogay-Tartar brought some green reed, and filled the pit, which was next covered with earth and made even; a stone was placed over the head of the dead man. After the soil had been well beaten down, all the Tartars again sat down in a row before the grave. There was a long pause.

„Allah! Allah! Allah!" They sighed, and rose.

The redbearded man distributed some money to the old men; then he took a lash, struck himself three times upon the forehead, and went home.

Next morning Gilin saw him leading a horse out of the village with three Tartars following behind. When they had come outside the village the redbearded man took off his undertunic, and tucked up his sleeves, revealing his strong arms; he drew out a dagger, and sharpened it on the whetstone. The Tartars held up the horse's head, and the redbearded man cut its throat, threw it down, and began to skin it with his huge hands. Some women and girls then washed the bowels, and intestines, and the horse was chopped up into large pieces and dragged into the hut. All the village gathered together at the hut of the redbearded man in memory of his dead brother.

Three days they ate the horseflesh and drank the booza. All the Tartars were at home. On the fourth day, in the afternoon, Gilin noticed that they were preparing for a journey. Horses were brought out, and ten men, the redbearded

Tartar included, started off; only Abdul remained at home. It was new moon, and the nights were still dark.

„Well", thought Gilin, „I must run off to day". He spoke to Kostilin about it, but Kostilin was apprehensive.

„How can we run off? we do not know the road".

„I know it".

„And besides, we shall not be able to reach the fortress in one night".

„If we do not get there, we can pass the night in the forest. I have stored up some flat cakes. Why should you remain here? Well if they send you the money from home, but perhaps they will not be able to get so much. And the Tartars are very angry just now because one of them has been killed by the Russians. I have heard that they intend killing us„.

Kostilin considered a little, and said:

„Well, let us go!"

V.

Gilin crept into the hole, and made it wider, to enable Kostilin to get through; then they sat waiting until all was quiet in the village. Now Gilin crawled under the wall, and got out. He whispered to Kostilin: „come!" Kostilin crawled also, but his foot caught a stone, and he made a noise. Their master had a watch dog, a fierce animal; it was called Ooliashin. Gilin had fed it before. Ooliashin heard the noise, began to bark, and ran up to them followed by other dogs. Gilin whistled gently, and threw a bit of flat cake to him. Ooliaschin recognized him, wagged his tail, and left off barking. The master heard the dog bark, and shouted at it from the hut.

Gilin meanwhile scratched the dog behind its ears; it stood quietly by rubbing itself against his legs and wagging its tail.

They crouched a short time behind the corner. All was silent again; you could only hear the cough of a sheep in the fold and the murmur of water running down over pebbles. It was dark; the stars were visible high up in the sky, and the new moon with her horns turned upwards looked red over the hill; the hollows were covered with white mist.

Gilin rose, and said to his companion:

„Well, friend, come along!"

They moved on. Scarcely had they proceeded a few steps, when they heard the Mollah singing: „Allah! Besmilla! Il-rachman!" which means: „people, come to the mosque!" Again they crouched hiding themselves under the wall. They waited until all the people had passed. At length all was still again.

„Come along now with God's help!"

They made the sign of the cross, and continued their way. They passed the yard, and descended a steep hill; when they came to a river, they crossed it, and then proceeded along a hollow. The mist below was very thick, but above their heads the stars were shining. Gilin noticed by the stars what direction to take. It was cool in the mist, and walking was easy, only their boots were uncomfortable: they were trodden down. Gilin took his off, threw them away, and continued his way barefooted. He leapt from stone to stone, and every now and then looked at the stars. Kostilin began to lag behind.

„Not so fast", he said, „these confounded boots rub my feet dreadfully".

— Take them off, you will find it easier.

Kostilin went on barefooted, but it was still worse: the stones cut his feet, and he still lagged behind. Gilin said:

„Don't mind hurting your feet, they will get well again, but if the Tartars reach us, we shall be killed; that's worse!"

Kostilin said nothing, he walked on moaning. They proceeded in the hollow for a long time. Suddenly they heard to their right dogs barking. Gilin stopped, looked round, and climbed up a hill.

„We have made a mistake", he said, „we have taken too much to the right; there is a village here, I have seen it from the mountain; we must go back, and then turn to the left up a hill. There must be a forest".

Kostilin said:

„Wait a little, let me take breath, my feet are bleeding".

„Never mind, friend; they will get well again; leap more lightly, so!"

And Gilin ran back, and then to the left up hill into the forest. Kostilin lagged behind, and moaned. Gilin whispered gently: „Hush, hush!" and continued to walk on.

They ascended the hill, and entered the forest, tearing their clothes with the thorns and prickles. They found a path, and proceeded along it.

„Stop!" The sound of horses' hoofs was heard on the road. They stood still, and listened. The sound ceased; they went on—the hoofs resounded again; when they stopped, the noise ceased. Gilin crawled to the roadside, and looked; there was something standing there; it was like a horse, and yet it was not a horse, some extraordinary object was upon it, not at all like a man; it snorted. „What miracle is this?" Gilin whistled gently, it rushed off to the forest; a cracking noise was heard, as though a storm had risen, and boughs were being broken by the wind.

Kostilin was greatly alarmed, but Gilin laughed, and said:

„It is a stag. Do you hear it crushing the boughs with its horns? We have been frightened by it, and it has been frightened by us".

They walked on again. Morning was approaching, and still they were not certain that they were on the right way. Gilin thought it was the same road by which he had been carried off, and that about ten versts still remained to the fortress; but there was no sure sign, and it was impossible to make out anything in the night. They now came to an open space. Kostilin sat down, and said:

„You may do as you like, but I am not able to reach our destination, my legs refuse to move".

Gilin tried to persuade him.

„No", said Kostilin, „I cannot go farther".

Gilin got angry, and scolded him.

„Well then, I shall go on alone, good bye!"

Kostilin rose and went on. They walked about four versts more. The mist in the forest had become still denser, you could see nothing around you, and the stars were now scarcely visible.

Suddenly they heard the tread of a horse in front of them; its hoofs struck the stones. Gilin lay down flat upon the ground, and listened.

„So it is, a rider is coming up to us!"

They ran off the road, sat down in the bushes, and waited. Gilin again crawled to the road side, and looked on. A Tartar on horseback was driving a cow and humming something under his nose. The Tartar passed by, and Gilin returned to Kostilin.

„Thank God! we are out of danger; get up, and come along!"

Kostilin tried to get up, but fell down again.

„I cannot, really I cannot! I have no more strength".

He was heavy and stout, and perspired profusely; the cold mist in the forest and his bleeding feet had made him feel quite faint. Gilin tried to lift him up, but Kostilin cried out:

„You pain me!"

Gilin was alarmed.

„Why do you shout so? the Tartar is near, he will hear us!" He thought: „He is decidedly very weak, what shall I do with him? it won't do to desert a comrade".

„Well", he said, „get up! if you are not able to walk, I shall carry you on my back".

He lifted Kostilin on his back, got out upon the road again, and went on.

„But for Heaven's sake don't press my throat with your hands, hold on by my shoulders".

It was a heavy burden for Gilin. He was himself weary, and his feet were bleeding; but still he continued to carry Kostilin along the road, every now and then adjusting him upon his back.

Kostilin's exclamation must have reached the ears of the Tartar, for Gilin soon heard some one riding behind them and calling in the Tartar dialect. Gilin rushed into the bushes. The Tartar drew his gun and fired, but he missed his mark, and rode off.

„We are lost, friend", said Gilin, „he will immediately call some Tartars together; and they will pursue us. If we do not succeed in getting three versts farther, we are lost". And in his inmost heart he thought: „why did I take this burden with me! if I were alone, I should have been safe by this time!"

Kostilin said:

„Go alone, why should you perish for my sake?"

— No, I shall not go, it would not be right to forsake a comrade.

He again lifted him upon his shoulders, and went on. He walked thus about a verst. They were still in the forest, and there was no outlet to be seen. The mist now began to disperse, clouds began to gather, and the stars were no more visible. Gilin was quite exhausted.

He came to a spring surrounded by stones; here he stopped, and let down Kostilin.

"Let me rest and have a drink here. We can also eat our flat cakes. The fortress cannot be far off now".

He had just bent down to drink, when he heard the sound of horses' feet behind. Again they both rushed into the bushes to their right hand, and lay down upon the ground behind an eminence.

They heard Tartar voices; the Tartars had stopped at the same place, where Gilin and Kostilin had turned off the road. After a short consultation they seemed to be setting their dogs on, and a strange dog rushing over bushes ran up to them, and began to bark.

Several Tartars, also strangers, now approached; they seized the two Russians, bound them, placed them on their horses, and carried them off.

When they had proceded about three versts, they met Abdul the master, accompanied by two Tartars. He said something to the Tartars, and Gilin and his companion were placed upon his horses, and carried back to the village.

Abdul did not laugh now, nor did he speak a word to them.

At dawn they were brought to the village and placed in the street. Boys came running up to them. They shouted, and struck them with stones and whips.

The Tartars assembled in a circle; the old man from the foot of the mountain came also. They began to converse. Gilin was able to make out that they were talking about them and considering what to do with them. Some said they must be carried away farther into the mountains, but the old man said: „They must be put to death". Abdul disputed with them saying: „I have paid money for them, and I want to get their ransom". But the old man said: „They will not pay anything, and they will only do some mischief. And besides it is a sin to feed Russians. They must be killed, that's all".

They dispersed. The master came up to Gilin, and said: „If in two weeks' time I receive no ransom for you, I shall whip you to death. And if you once more attempt to escape, I shall kill you like dogs. Write a letter and write well".

Some paper was brought to them, and they wrote letters. The footblocks were again put on, and they were led to the mosque, behind which there was a pit five arshines deep; into this pit they were let down.

VI.

They had a bad time of it now. Their footblocks were never taken off, and they were never lifted out of their pit. They received for food some unbaked paste, which was thrown down to them like unto dogs, and some water in a pitcher. The pit was filthy, stifling and wet. Kostilin felt quite ill: he had swellings and a pain in all his body; he either moaned or slept. Gilin also felt depressed; he saw that their situation was very bad, and he knew not how to get away.

He attempted to dig a passage under ground, but he had nowhere to throw the earth; his master saw what he was doing, and threatened to kill him.

He was one day sitting in the pit, thinking of freedom, and felt very dull. Suddenly a flat cake came falling into his lap, then another, followed by some cherries. He raised his head — there was Dina. She looked down upon him, laughed, and ran away. Gilin thought: „Perhaps Dina might help us?"

He then cleared a space in the pit, got out some clay, and set to making dolls. He made figures of men, horses and dogs, and resolved to throw them up to Dina, if she should come again.

But Dina did not come the next day.

Meanwhile Gilin heard the noise of horses' feet; some people rode by, and the Tartars gathered together near to the mosque; they disputed, shouted, and spoke something about the Russians. He also heard the old man's voice. He could not well make out what they were saying, but he conjectured that the Russians had come near, and that the Tartars were afraid they would enter their village, and were at a loss what to do with the captives.

Having talked some time they went away. Suddenly Gilin heard a rustling noise above. He looked up, and saw Dina squatting at the edge of the pit, her knees higher than her head; she bent down, her necklace dangled over the pit. Her eyes sparkled like stars. She took out of her sleeve two cheese cakes, and threw them to him. Gilin took them, and said: „Why did you not come so long? I have made some playthings for you, there! and he threw them up to her one by one. But she shook her head, and would not look at them. „I do not want them", she said. She was silent a short time, and then she spoke again: "John, they want to kill you". Saying this she made a sign with her hand upon her throat.

— Who wants to kill me?

— My father; the old men order him to do it. I am sorry for you.

Gilin said:

"If you pity me, bring me a long pole".

She shook her head to say she could not do it. He folded his hands, and implored her:

"Dina, I pray you, dear Dina, do bring it!"

"I cannot", she said, "they will see; they are all at home". And she went away.

In the evening Gilin was sitting and thinking. Every now and then he looked up. The stars were visible, but the moon had not risen yet. The Mollah shouted out, and then all was still again. Gilin was beginning to slumber, he thought the girl would not have the courage to do it.

Suddenly he felt some clay falling upon his head; he looked up — a long pole was touching the other side of the pit; by and by it began to descend slowly into the pit. Gilin was very glad, he seized it, and pulled it down; it was a strong pole; he had seen it before upon his master's roof.

He looked up, and saw the stars shining high up in the sky, and just over the pit Dina's eyes were sparkling in the darkness like the eyes of a cat. She bent her head over the pit, and whispered:

"John! John!" and made signs to be as quiet as possible.

"What?" said Gilin.

— They are all gone away, only two are at home.

Gilin said:

"Kostilin, come! let us make a last attempt, I shall help you up".

Kostilin would not listen to him.

„No", he said, „I suppose I am not destined to get away from here. How can I go, when I have no strength to move?"

— Well then good bye, do not think ill of me!" And he kissed Kostilin.

He then seized the pole, told Dina to hold it tightly and began to climb up. Once or twice he slipped down, the footblock hindered him greatly. Kostilin supported him a little, and at last he was at the top. Dina pulled him by the shirt with her tiny hands, and laughed.

Gilin gave her the pole, and said:

„Take it back, Dina; if they miss it, they will punish you".

She dragged away the pole, and Gilin went down the hill. When he had descended, he took a sharp stone, and attempted to knock off the lock of the footblock; the lock was strong, and he could not manage it. He heard some one bounding lightly down the hill. He thought: „It must be Dina again". And so it was. She took the stone, and said.

„Let me do it!"

She kneeled down, and set to work. But her little hands, as thin as twigs, had no strength in them. She threw away the stone, and wept. Gilin tried again, and Dina squatted down beside him holding him by the shoulder. Gilin turned round, and saw to his left behind the hill a red streak in the sky: it was the moon rising. „Well", he thought, „I must pass the glen and reach the forest before the moon is up". He rose, and threw away the stone. He must proceed with the footblock on.

„Good bye, little Dina", he said, „I shall never forget you".

Dina held him fast, and tried to find a place for some flat cakes; he took them.

„Thank you", he said, „you are a good girl! Who will

make dolls for you when I am gone?" and he patted her on the head.

Dina wept bitterly; she covered her face with her hands, and ran up the hill bounding like a goat. You could hear the coins in her tresses rattling upon her back.

Gilin crossed himself; he took hold of the lock in the footblock that it should not rattle, and went along the road dragging his foot and every now and then looking at the place where the moon was rising. He recognized the road; he had about eight versts to go in a straight line. If only he could manage to reach the forest before the moon had quite risen. He crossed the river; the sky was beginning to look white behind the hill. He proceeded in a glen, turning back to see if the moon was appearing. The red streak in the sky had now become light, and one side of the glen was also becoming lighter and lighter. The shade from the hill was creeping nearer and nearer to him.

Gilin kept in the shade. He made haste, but the moon was rising rapidly; the tops of the trees to the right hand were now also lit up. By the time he approached the forest the moon had risen over the mountains, it was now as light as day. You could distinguish all the leaves on the trees; profound silence reigned around, only the murmur of a rivulet down below was heard.

Gilin reached the forest without meeting anybody. He found a dark place there, and sat down to rest.

Having rested and eaten a flat cake he found a stone and again attempted to knock off the footblock. His hands were all bruised, but he could not get rid of it. He rose, and continued his way. He walked about a verst; he was now tired out, and his feet ached; he was obliged to halt after every few steps. „There is no help for it", he thought, „I must drag myself along, till I have no more strength left in me; if I sit down, I shall not be able to get up again. I shall not reach the fortress this night; as soon as it begins to dawn, I shall lie down in the forest and spend the day there; in the night I shall walk on again".

Gilin continued walking all night; he met only two Tartars on horseback, but he heard them at a distance, and hid himself behind a tree.

The moon was already beginning to look paler, the dew had fallen, it was not far from dawn, and Gilin had not yet reached the edge of the forest. „I shall make thirty steps more", he thought, „and then I shall turn off the road into the forest and sit down there". When he had made thirty steps, he saw that he was coming to the end of the forest. It was quite light outside; he could see plainly the steppe and the fortress, and to the left, quite near, under the hill there were fires burning; some of them were going out, and the smoke was spreading over the surface of the earth; he could also see some people near to the woodpiles.

He looked attentively, and saw Cossacks, soldiers and the glitter of rifles.

Gilin rejoiced greatly; he gathered up his remaining strength, and went down hill. „If a mounted Tartar sees me here in the open field", he thought, „I shall not be able to escape, although the fortress is so near".

Just as he was thinking thus, he noticed to the left three Tartars standing upon a hillock. They perceived him, and rushed towards him. His heart sank. He waved his hands, and shouted with all his might:

„Friends, brothers, help me!"

His people heard him; some mounted Cossacks rode towards him so as to intercept the Tartars.

It was a longer way for the Cossacks than for the Tartars. But Gilin gathered all his strength, took up the footblock in his hand, and ran towards the Cossacks, crossing himself and crying out:

„Brothers! brothers! brothers!"

There were fifteen Cossacks. The Tartars were frightened, and began to halt one by one.

And Gilin ran up to the Cossacks.

The Cossacks surrounded him enquiring who he was, and where he came from. Gilin was nearly out of his wits; he could only cry, and repeat:

„Brothers! brothers!"

The soldiers also gathered round Gilin; some brought him bread, others gruel or gin; some covered him with their cloaks, others knocked off the footblock.

The officers recognized him, they took him to the fortress; the soldiers and his comrades rejoiced, and gathered around him.

Gilin told all that had befallen him, adding:

„This is then what happened to me instead of my going home and marrying; well, I suppose it was not to be!"

He remained serving in the Caucasus.

Kostilin was let free for a ransom of five thousand roubles only a month later; he was brought back more dead than alive.

Printed by Libri Plureos GmbH in Hamburg,
Germany